WYM/CH

Please return / renew by
You can renew it at:
norlink.norfolk.gov.uk
or by telephone: 0344 800 8006
Please have your library card & PIN ready

NORFOLK LIBRARY
AND INFORMATION SERVICE

Henry's House

EGYptians

Philip Ardagh

illustrated by Mike Gordon

SCHOLASTIC

**In memory of Spoons –
Jill and Steve's very special cat.**
P.A.

Consultant: Dr Kathryn E Piquette,
Institute of Archaeology, University of London

Editorial Director: Lisa Edwards
Senior Editor: Jill Sawyer

Scholastic Children's Books,
Euston House, 24 Eversholt Street,
London NW1 1DB, UK
a division of Scholastic Ltd
London ~ New York ~ Toronto ~ Sydney ~ Auckland
Mexico City ~ New Delhi ~ Hong Kong

First published in the UK by Scholastic Ltd, 2009

ISBN 978 1407 10720 2

Printed and bound by Tien Wah Press Pte. Ltd, Singapore

10 9 8 7 6 5 4 3 2 1

Philip Ardagh and Mike Gordon are regular visitors to Henry's House. Philip (the one with the beard) keeps a note of everything that's going on, and even reads a mind or two. Mike (the one without the beard) sketches whatever he sees, however fantastical it may be ... and together they bring you the adventures of Henry, an ordinary boy in an extraordinary house!

Contents

Welcome to Henry's House!

Hi, I'm Henry! Welcome to my house. Anything can happen here and it often does.

I like finding things out, and so does my dog Mothball...

I like FOOD too!

FISHCAKE

You never know what's behind the next door or just around the corner, but Jaggers the caretaker usually keeps an eye on things.

That's true! I do.

Then there are the guests ... and not all of us are human.

No wonder every day is such a big adventure!

Into the past

7

Meet the Pharaoh

That's my father over there. The hat on his head is his crown.

Why is he holding those funny-looking things?

The crook shows he guides his people. The flail shows his strength and power.

Bata and his family are from the New Kingdom period of ancient Egyptian history (over 3,000 years ago).

A red-and-white crown like this is called a double crown.

Wearing a double crown means that the Pharaoh rules both Upper AND Lower Egypt.

CROOK

FLAIL

On ancient Egyptian statues, carvings and paintings kings were always shown with beards.

It was a symbol of just how important the king was.

The king's beard wasn't real.

Why's that woman fanning Bata's dad with ostrich feathers? Couldn't they just turn the heating down?

Even some female Pharaohs wore fake beards!

9

Royalty on the move

This is my mother. Mum, this is Henry.

I love your house, Henry. But we have made a few changes to our rooms!

HEY! Isn't someone going to introduce ME?

Your father and I are about to go out, Bata. That's why we are dressed in all our finery.

I'm sure Her Majesty has been eating too many figs!

My father has many wives, but only my mother is queen. She is the daughter of the last king.

PUFF!

PANT!

The queen often travelled in a special chair called a litter.

Pyramid power

Bata! Look! There's a pyramid being built in my back garden!

Incredible! Our people stopped building pyramids a long, long time before my father became Pharaoh.

There are hundreds of people swarming around like ants!

Teams of men pulled stones up huge ramps on wooden rollers.

Carpenters made rollers from logs.

The ancient Egyptians only built pyramids in the early part of their long history.

The ramps were made from mud. These were raised as the pyramid got taller.

Most of the workmen were not slaves. They were farmers.

RAMP

Stone was brought on boats on the River Nile.

Stone masons cut the stones just the right size and shape.

The biggest and most famous pyramid is the Great Pyramid at Giza.

The pyramid is made up of over two million stone blocks.

It is the biggest stone building EVER built.

It was built over 4,500 years ago for a king called Cheops.

Today, most of its smooth limestone covering has gone.

It is 146 metres high.

GREAT PYRAMID

Pyramids may have been built in this shape to look like the sun's rays.

Mummy!

Take a look at this. Inside this coffin is the dead king's bandaged body.

His body has been treated in a special way to stop it rotting.

Stop staring at me!

WADJET EYE

This symbol of an eye was thought to protect everything near it.

Some of the body's inside bits were taken out and put in special jars.

CANOPIC JARS

Next, the body was filled with:
• sawdust to soak up the juices and fill it out
• herbs to hide any nasty smells
• salt to stop it rotting.

DEATH MASK (BANDAGES UNDERNEATH)

GOOD-LUCK CHARMS WERE TUCKED INSIDE

I wonder where this leads?

FIRE DOOR

Later, the body was bandaged up and a death mask put on top.

Life after death

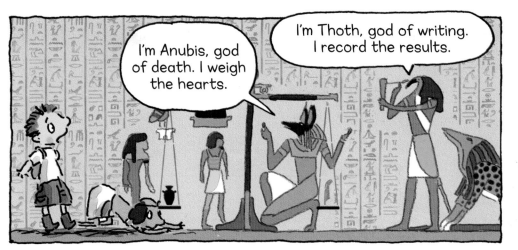

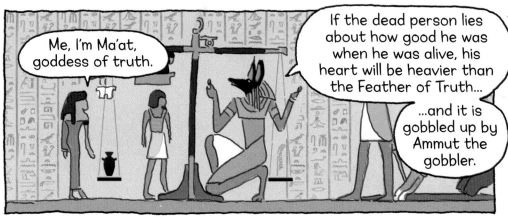

19

Gods and goddesses

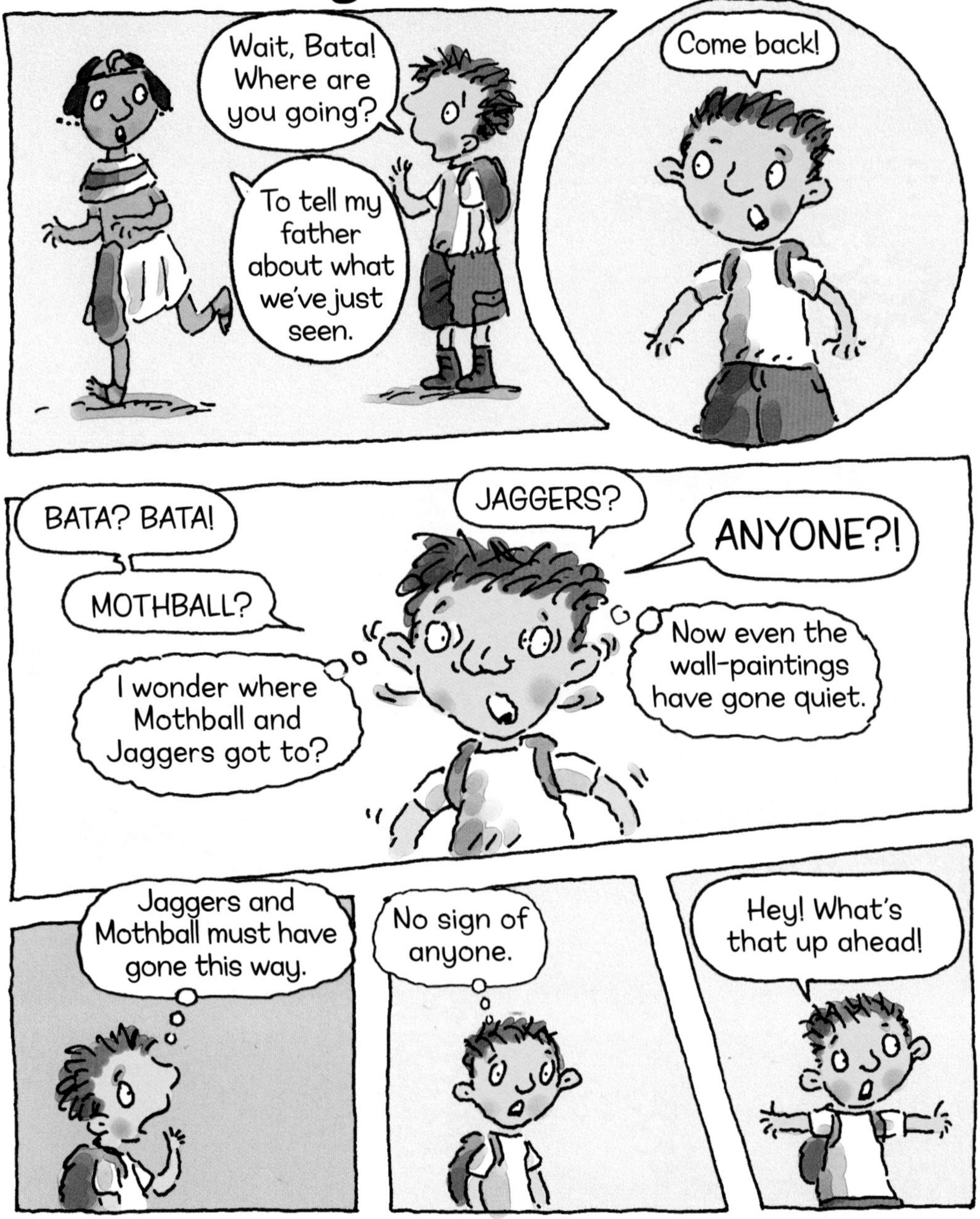

21

THE SUN GOD, THE LIONESS AND THE RIVER NILE

Re made the human race and, as long as people worshipped him and were afraid of him, he was happy to let them live their lives.

Over time, however, some people stopped worshipping him. They stopped being afraid. They thought the sun god must be old and weak.

Re got very angry. He sent his daughter Hathor down to Earth to kill the ones who had stopped worshipping him. Hathor appeared in the shape of a huge lioness and killed her father's enemies. But she didn't stop because she now loved the taste of human blood.

Re had to act fast. He flooded the land with a strong red beer. Hathor thought it was blood and drank it. The beer made her happy, then sleepy and she went home. The human race was saved.

Even to this day, the River Nile sometimes flows red.

This is a scarab beetle. The scarab was a symbol of the god Re. Re was said to roll the sun across the sky. Scarabs are also called dung beetles because they roll balls of dung – animal poo – across the ground.

Write on!

We know these stories today because they were written down.

The ancient Egyptian alphabet is very different to ours. They used pictures. Our alphabet has 26 letters. Theirs ended up with over 6,000!

Words written with pictures are called hieroglyphs (hire-o-gliffs).

The pictures were used in different ways.

Some stand for the things they actually looked like.

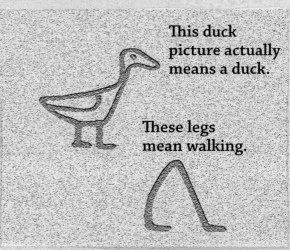

This duck picture actually means a duck.

These legs mean walking.

Some pictures stand for sounds in the same way that letters do in our own alphabet.

Here's an alphabet of "sound pictures" put together by modern-day experts.

EGYPTIAN ALPHABET

a	g	n	th
ah	g/j	o	u
b	h or	oo	v
c	i	p	w
ch	j/g	qu	
d	k	r	x
e	kh	s	
ee	l	sh	y
f, ph	m	t	z

You could write your own messages using this, Henry!

But you'll need a few important tips first...

Carved in stone

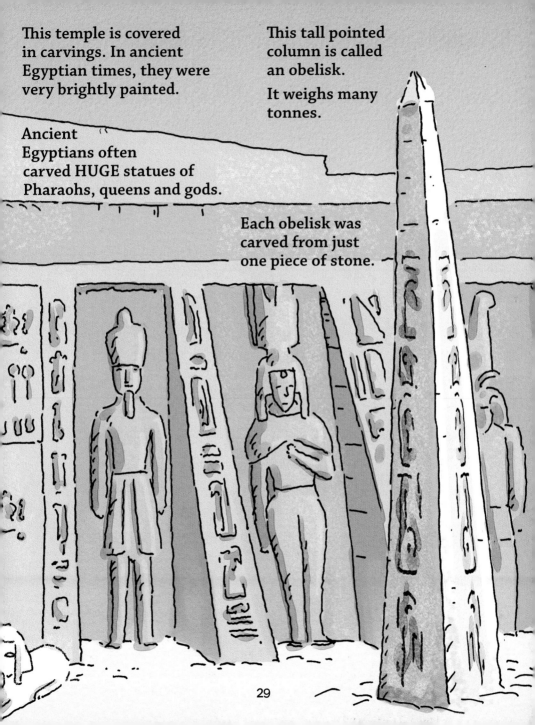

This temple is covered in carvings. In ancient Egyptian times, they were very brightly painted.

This tall pointed column is called an obelisk.

It weighs many tonnes.

Ancient Egyptians often carved HUGE statues of Pharaohs, queens and gods.

Each obelisk was carved from just one piece of stone.

All aboard!

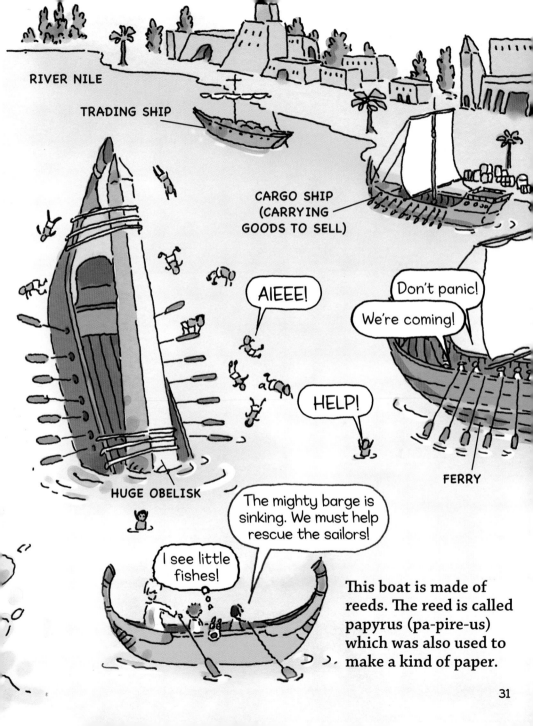

RIVER NILE

TRADING SHIP

CARGO SHIP
(CARRYING
GOODS TO SELL)

AIEEE!

Don't panic!

We're coming!

HELP!

HUGE OBELISK

FERRY

The mighty barge is sinking. We must help rescue the sailors!

I see little fishes!

This boat is made of reeds. The reed is called papyrus (pa-pire-us) which was also used to make a kind of paper.

Working the soil

The River Nile flooded the land once a year. It left behind a layer of good soil. Without this soil, the land would be a sandy desert.

Ditches were dug so that water would flow to where it was most needed.

Ancient Egyptians planted crops to feed animals and people.

FLAX FOR MAKING CLOTHES AND ROPE

DITCH

BARLEY FOR BREAD AND BEER

GEESE

GOATS

RIVER NILE

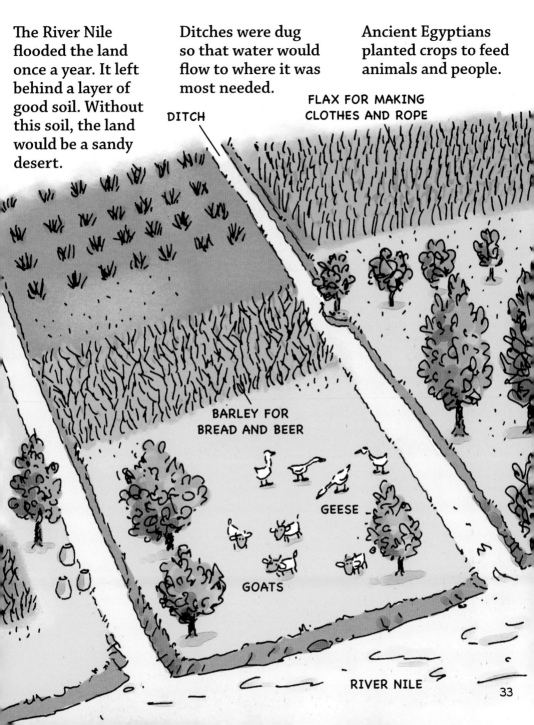

Food glorious food!

37

Home sweet home

Ah, there you all are. You'll never believe it...

There's a bunch of people running about the house dressed as ancient Egyptians!

I think you'll find that they ARE ancient Egyptians, Professor!

Poppycock and piffle, young man!

Surely you've noticed that Henry's House isn't – er – quite like other houses, Prof?

Which brings me to the changes I'd like to make to my room.

I'd like to make it more like an ancient Egyptian villa...

I've made some sketches.

IMPORTANT PARTS OF A RICH EGYPTIAN'S VILLA
(All houses built with mud bricks and painted plaster.)

GUARD

GATEHOUSE

A guarded gatehouse to keep out unwanted visitors.

Stable for horses, donkeys and chariots.

GRAIN STORES

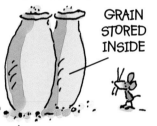

GRAIN STORED INSIDE

TOMORROW'S FISH SUPPER

A fishpond in the middle of the garden. Nice to look at and a good supply of fresh food.

SMALL WINDOWS TO KEEP OUT THE SUN

The kitchens are well away from the main house.

PLENTY OF COLUMNS

Main hall: richly decorated. Ideal for banquets.

Looking good!

Poorer people didn't live in such grand places. Most ancient Egyptians lived in one or two simple rooms.

I'm not sure Henry's dad will let you dig a fishpond!

It was the same with clothes and jewellery. The rich had lots more of it and it was much better made!

Men and women often drew around their eyes with special black paint called kohl (coll).

It not only looked nice, it probably helped keep flies away too!

They also liked to redden their cheeks and lips.

Because it was often hot, people didn't want to wear many clothes.

They often walked barefoot or wore sandals.

Some rich people shaved their hair off (to keep cool) then wore wigs when they needed to look smart.

RINGS

Beaded collars were popular with men and women.

MIRROR OF POLISHED METAL

BEADED COLLAR

GLASS BEADS

Some people padded their hair to make it look "bigger" for big occasions!

BRACELETS

Both men and women rubbed in perfumed oils.

CLOAK

Most of the time, people wore simple white clothes made from a plant called flax.

41

Party!

It's been a long day, Mothball. Let's go to bed.

After another quick snack?

WAG! WAG!

Goodnight, Professor!

Goodnight, Henry.

Goodnight, Cookie!

Goodnight, Henry.

Goodnight, Hank!

Goodnight, Henry!

Goodnight, Jaggers!

Sleep well, Henry.

A little later...

What's all that noise?

It's probably my tummy rumbling.

What a racket!

KNOCK! KNOCK! KNOCK!

This is CRAZY. There's a trap door down here!

Hello, Henry! Come and join the party...

42

On the river

You ancient Egyptians know how to party, Bata!

I'm STUFFED full!

They love animals. One guest had a pet monkey, another talked about his cats and snakes ... but us DOGS were the most popular by far!

The next day...

People enjoyed hunting birds as well as hippos.

Some used their pet cats to frighten the birds out of the reeds.

HUNTING SPEAR

NET TO CATCH BIRDS IN

PAPYRUS REEDS

Trying to tip over your opponent's boat was also fun.

These boats were made from papyrus reeds.

PUNTING POLE, TO PUSH BOAT ALONG

Kids

I didn't see any kids fishing or hunting. What do you get up to?

DROOL!

Lots of different fun and games, Henry.

Take your pick.

Balls were made from wood, clay, leather or even plants.

CLAY SPINNING TOPS

This wooden horse on wheels was made over 2,000 years ago.

Pull the string on this toy cat and its jaws snapped shut.

STRING

PEG TEETH

You guys certainly do lots of different stuff.

Children's hair was usually shaved off, except for a long braid down one side.

Girls played with clay or wooden dolls.

Children often helped around the farm, home or workshop.

Children's pets included cats, dogs, geese and even monkeys.

Most children didn't go to school. Those who did were usually boys.

They came from the richer families.

Girls were often taught at home. Lessons included music and writing.

47

Army on the move

An army on the move could quickly set up camp each day.

Take a look at my model army camp and soldiers, Henry.

The walls were made of soldiers' shields.

Officers slept in tents.

GUARDED ENTRANCE

This soldier is wearing leather armour.

PROPERTY OF BATA

Doctors were there to help the wounded.

Valley of the Kings

I hope to ride into battle on a chariot one day.

In the meantime, do you want to see some pictures I found on the computer, Bata?

Computer?

I'll show you.

Stop chewing that soldier, Mothball!

During the time of the New Kingdom, Pharaohs were not buried in pyramids, but here in the Valley of the Kings.

This is what it looks like nowadays, Bata.

Everything had been stolen from the pyramids a long time before. These tombs in the valley were thought to be safer from robbers. Many were cut into the hillside.

One of the most famous tombs is that of Tutankhamun...

The most famous find was his solid gold death mask.

It weighs 11 kg.

I know all about him, Henry!

King Tut

Tutankhamun was born in around 1347 BC. He became king when he was about ten.

Can someone find me a smaller crown and throne, please?

SWING! SWING!

Because he was just a boy, two grown-ups ruled for him:

Are you Ay?

Aye, I am!

AY

HOREMHEB

He married a princess called Ankhesenamun.

That makes me QUEEN!

Sadly, Tutankhamun died when he was about nineteen.

Ugh! I don't feel like getting up.

Typical teenager!

Ay then married Ankhesenamun and became the new Pharaoh!

TUT! TUT!

Tutankhamun was buried in a tomb originally meant for someone else.

His body was mummified then placed in a gold coffin, two wooden outer coffins and a stone sarcophagus (sar-coff-a-guss).

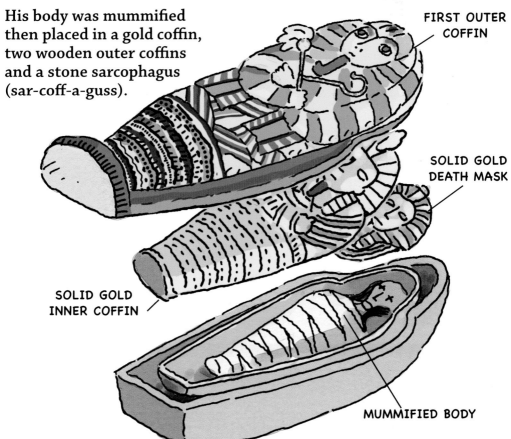

FIRST OUTER COFFIN

SOLID GOLD DEATH MASK

SOLID GOLD INNER COFFIN

MUMMIFIED BODY

An amazing find

Henry has been sucked into Egypt and back to 26 November 1922!

LORD CARNARVON

HOWARD CARTER

THE MUMMY'S CURSE?

A number of amazing coincidences and unfortunate events surround the discovery of Tutankhamun's tomb.

On the day the tomb was opened, Howard Carter's pet canary was eaten by a cobra. (There's a golden cobra on Tutankhamun's death mask.)

Lord Carnarvon died just five months later. At the moment he died it is said that his dog dropped dead back in England and all the lights went out in Egypt's capital city, Cairo.

An X-ray specialist died on the way to study the mummified body.

Jay Gould, an important American businessman, visited Tutankhamun's tomb, caught a cold that turned into pneumonia – which killed him!

The Egyptian Ali Kemel Fahmy Bey visited the tomb then was shot dead by his wife at the Savoy Hotel in London.

Six people who had been at the opening of the tomb were dead within ten years.

BUT ... twenty other people who'd been there were all fine! Howard Carter lived for many more years, dying aged 64.

Timeline

ANCIENT EGYPTIAN CIVILIZATION

4000 BC   3000 BC   2000 BC   1000 BC

3100 BC
ANCIENT EGYPTIAN
CIVILIZATION

HIEROGLYPHS INVENTED

AGE OF THE
GREAT PHARAOHS

THE GREAT PYRAMID
AT GIZA BUILT

Later that evening...

The pyramid has gone from the garden and the River Nile's gone from the hallway.

I wonder if I'll ever run into Bata again?

You never know, Henry. Goodnight!

Glossary

Afterlife: the life ancient Egyptians believed that people had after they died.

Chariot: a small, speedy cart, pulled by horses and ridden standing up. It was often used in battle, with a driver and an archer (with his bow and arrows).

Crook: a long rod with a hook-shaped end. A Pharaoh carried a crook to show that he was the leader of his people.

Death mask: a solid mask placed over a mummy's face. Sometimes the mask was carved or painted to look like the face of the dead person. Tutankhamun's death mask was made of gold.

Flail: a rod with three strands at the end. Pharaohs held them to show their great power.

Flax: a plant that was used to make cloth for clothes.

Limestone: a kind of soft rock cut into stone blocks and used as covering for some pyramids. Most of the limestone has worn away to show the harder stones underneath.

Mummified body: a body which has been made into a mummy.

Mummy: a dead body which has been treated in a special way and wrapped in cloth so that it will last a long time.

Pharaoh: the title given to some ancient Egyptian kings (and a few queens).

Scribe: an official writer (at a time when very few people could read or write).

Shrine: a small holy building used as a place of worship.

Slaves: people "owned" by other people and forced to work without any pay. They were often captured foreigners.

Stonemason: a skilled craftsman who cuts and shapes stone.

Tombs: rooms where the dead are buried. Ancient Egyptian royal tombs were filled with everything the dead might need in the Afterlife. Pyramids are large tombs.

Valley of the Kings: a valley in Egypt where hundreds of tombs were built for dead kings and other important people.

Wadjet eye: a special eye-shaped sign meant to bring good luck and keep you safe.

Index

Henry's House

We hope you enjoyed your visit

to **Henry's House**

Come back soon!

Look out for:
- **Bodies**
- **Creepy-crawlies**
- **Dinosaurs**
- **Knights and Castles**
- **Space**